Working Scientifically

USING MODELS AND MATHS IN SCIENCE

by Riley Flynn

Raintree is an imprint of Capstone Global Library Limited, a company incorporated in England and Wales having its registered office at 264 Banbury Road, Oxford, OX2 7DY – Registered company number: 6695582

www.raintree.co.uk
myorders@raintree.co.uk

Edited by Anna Butzer
Designed by Sarah Bennett
Picture research by Eric Gohl
Production by Laura Manthe

ISBN 978 1 4747 2259 9 (hardback)
20 19 18 17 16
10 9 8 7 6 5 4 3 2 1

ISBN 978 1 4747 2283 4 (paperback)
21 20 19 18 17
10 9 8 7 6 5 4 3 2 1

British Library Cataloguing in Publication Data
A full catalogue record for this book is available from the British Library.

Every effort has been made to contact copyright holders of material reproduced in this book. Any omissions will be rectified in subsequent printings if notice is given to the publisher.

All the internet addresses (URLs) given in this book were valid at the time of going to press. However, due to the dynamic nature of the internet, some addresses may have changed, or sites may have changed or ceased to exist since publication. While the author and publisher regret any inconvenience this may cause readers, no responsibility for any such changes can be accepted by either the author or the publisher.

Acknowledgements
iStockphoto: busypix, 5; Shutterstock: conrado, 11, bluehand, 9, marybethcharles, 20, Paul Aniszewski, 17, Pavel L Photo and Video, 7, PhotoUG, 13, Tonello Photography, 19, Vladimir Wrangel, 15, wavebreakmedia, cover
Design Elements: Shutterstock

Printed and bound in the United Kingdom.

Contents

What is a model?

This is a model of a volcano.

Models look like real objects

or events. They help us

to understand how things work.

Models also help us to solve problems. There is a problem with the model of this car. Someone looks at the problem and fixes it. They build a real car that works.

Types of model

Some models show small or large copies of something. A globe is a small model of Earth. A solar system model shows the planets that circle the Sun.

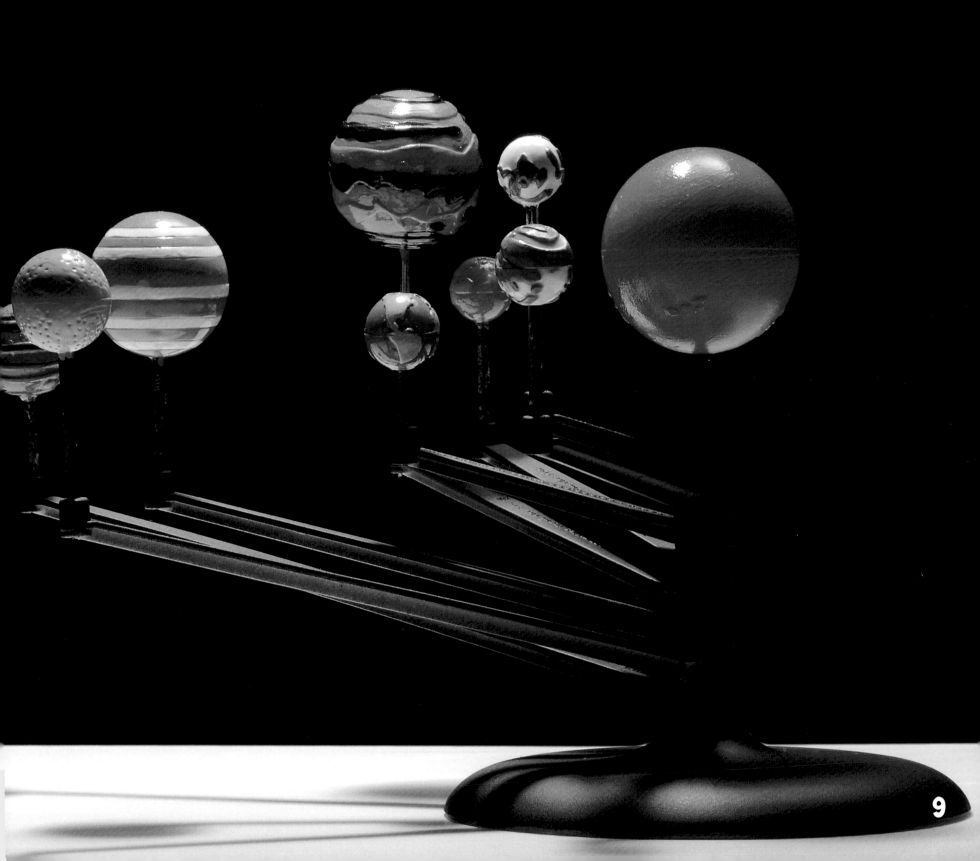

Other models help us to test objects. Engineers use crash tests to see how their car designs handle crashes. These tests are models that show if cars are safe.

Using maths

Maths can be used to model and describe things. Maths shows us how to use numbers. We use numbers to count and measure. Numbers can show us patterns.

You see two camels at the zoo.

One camel has one hump.

The other camel has two humps.

You can describe a camel by the
number of humps it has.

Finding patterns

Patterns repeat an order of things. Patterns are all around us. Look at a spider's web. Can you see a pattern?

Look at the rings in a tree stump. Can you see a pattern? You can discover the age of a tree by counting these rings. Each ring equals one year.

Using models

What type of house will be most likely to survive a hurricane or flood?

What you need:

- large, deep tray
- small wooden blocks
- small, smooth stones
- modelling clay and rolling pin
- plastic knife
- fan
- large jug of water
- an adult to help you

What to do:

1. Build three houses on the tray. Each house should be the same height. Use the wooden blocks to build the first house.

2. Build the second house out of stones.

3. Roll out the modelling clay. Then cut it into small rectangles. Build the third house out of modelling clay.

4. Place a fan in front of the houses. Turn it on low. Did any of the houses fall down?

5. Turn the fan up to medium. Observe.

6. Turn the fan up to high. Now did any of the houses fall? Which house stood for the longest?

7. Put the fan away. Repeat steps 1–3. Pour water into the tray. Did any of the houses collapse?

What do you think now?

Make a claim. A claim is something you believe to be true. What have you learned from these models?

Glossary

describe give information about something

engineer person who uses science and maths to plan, design or build

equal same as something else in size, number or value

measure find out the size or strength of something

model small copy or design of an object

pattern repeating arrangement of colours and shapes

Read more

The Big Book of Science: Things to Make and Do (Usborne Activities), Rebecca Gilpin (Usborne Publishing, 2012)

Experiments with Forces (Read and Experiment), Isabel Thomas (Raintree, 2015)

Websites

www.bbc.co.uk/bitesize/ks1/science
Enjoy some fun activities and learn more about science.

www.dkfindout.com/uk/science
Find out more about science and famous scientists.

Comprehension questions

1. Look at pages 17 and 19. Can you think of other places where you have seen patterns?

2. Describe two ways that scientists and engineers use models.

Index

Ladybird books are widely available, but in case of difficulty may be ordered by post or telephone from:

Ladybird Books – Cash Sales Department Littlegate Road Paignton Devon TQ3 3BE
Telephone 01803 554761

A catalogue record for this book is available from the British Library

Published by Ladybird Books Ltd Loughborough Leicestershire UK
Ladybird Books Ltd is a subsidiary of the Penguin Group of companies
Illustrations © Cliff Wright MCMXCVI
Text © Phil McMylor MCMXCVI
The author/artist have asserted their moral rights

LADYBIRD and the device of a Ladybird are trademarks of Ladybird Books Ltd

This way
Little Badger

by Phil McMylor
illustrated by Cliff Wright

The day was ending in the big wood.

Someone moved through the trees,
going very slowly…
searching high and low…
Little Badger and his sister, Belle.

Sister Belle knew the big wood well.
But everything was new
to Little Badger,
who had never in his life
been there before.

"Dig, Little Badger,"
said Sister Belle.
"A badger's claws
are made for digging!"

Sister Belle had big, strong
claws, but Little Badger's
claws were small and soft.

The sun went down behind the trees.

"Keep close,"
said Sister Belle.
"The dark is coming."

But, when Sister Belle stopped
to eat a fat white grub,
Little Badger went off on his own
and was soon lost.

Owl swooped down from
the great oak tree and hooted,
"Hurry home, Little Badger!"

"But which way is home?"
cried Little Badger.
"Oh, I wish Sister Belle was
here to show me the way!"

"This way, Little Badger!"
called a voice in the bushes.

Little Badger snuffled deeper
into the wood.

"You're not Sister Belle!"
said Little Badger when he saw…

Rabbit.

"Watch out, the dark is coming!"
said Rabbit.

"Can I see it?"
asked Little Badger.

"No, but it can see you!
It has lots of eyes,"
answered Rabbit.
And he hopped into his burrow.

"This way, Little Badger!"
called a voice in the branches.

Little Badger snuffled deeper
into the wood.

"You're not Sister Belle,"
said Little Badger when he saw…

Magpie.

"Watch out, the dark is coming!"
said Magpie.

"Can I talk to it?"
asked Little Badger.

"No, but it can talk to you!
It has lots of voices,"
answered Magpie.
And she flew into her nest.

"This way, Little Badger!"
called a voice in the wet leaves.

Little Badger snuffled deeper
into the wood.

"You're not Sister Belle!"
said Little Badger when he saw…

Mouse.

"Watch out, the dark is coming!"
said Mouse.

"Can I touch it?"
asked Little Badger.

"No, but it can touch you!
It has lots of fingers,"
answered Mouse.
And he ran into his hole.

"What does the dark do when it comes into the wood?" asked Little Badger.

"It chases the daylight away," called Mouse from his hole.

"It fills in the spaces between the branches and the leaves," called Magpie from her nest.

"It makes it hard to see," called Rabbit from his burrow.

"Owl can see!" squeaked Mouse, trembling.

A voice from the edge
of the wood called,
"This way, Little Badger!"

"Is that you, Dark?"
called Little Badger.
But, only an echo answered...
DARK... DARK... DARK!

Owl flew off.
The other animals hid.
And Little Badger...

ran away.

He saw lots of eyes…
and he heard lots of voices.
He felt lots of fingers…
tugging at his fur.

He hid in a deep, inky hole.

Little Badger whispered,
"Are you there, Dark?"

But only an echo answered...
DARK... DARK... DARK!

He tried to scramble out.
But the walls fell in.
Tree roots and damp earth
covered him from snout to tail.

"Dark has caught me!"
cried Little Badger.

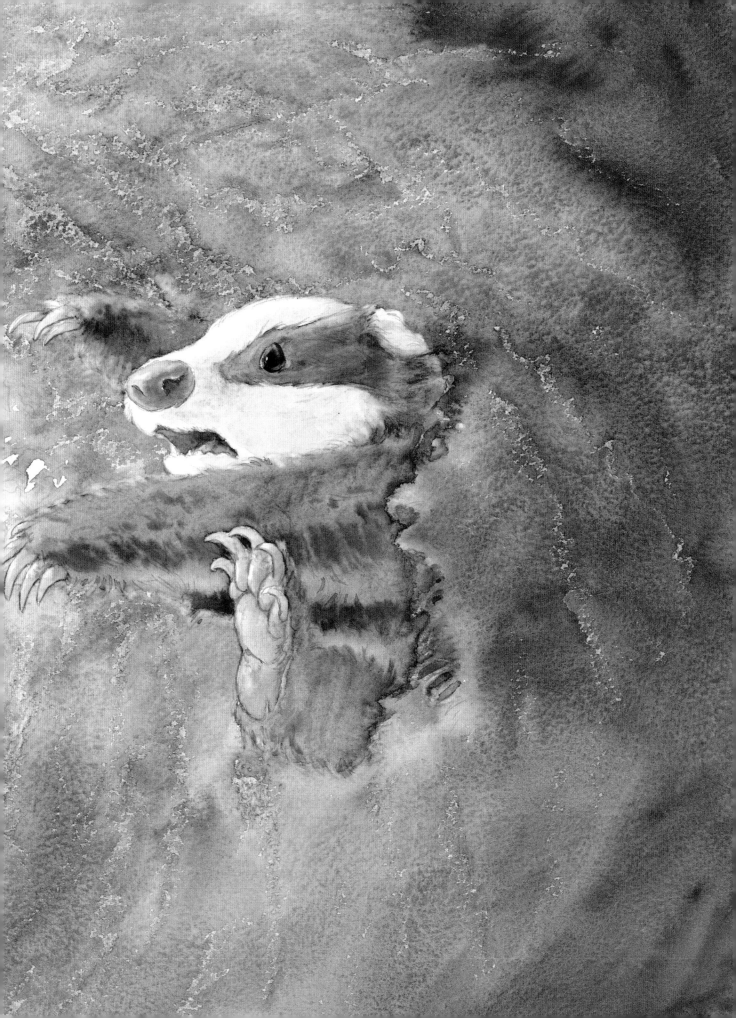

As he lay with the dark all about him,
Little Badger remembered what
Sister Belle had said:
A badger's claws are made for digging!

And Little Badger started to dig…
DIG… DIG… DIG!

And he didn't stop digging until he
was out of that deep, inky hole.

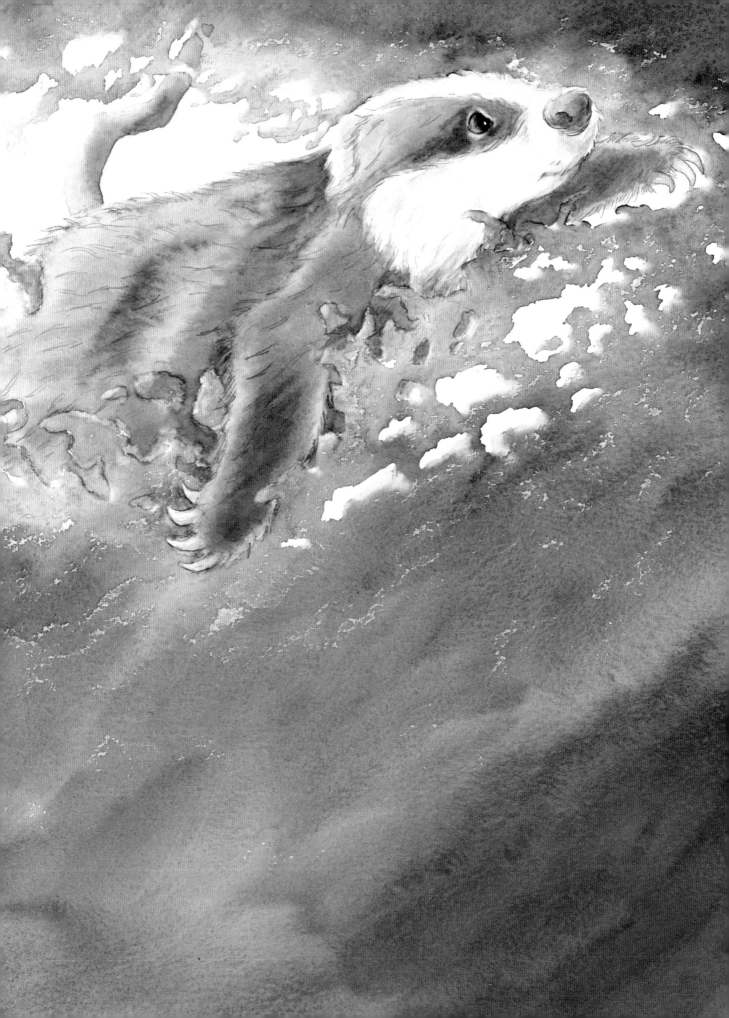

Little Badger shook the dirt out of
his eyes.

Someone moved through the trees,
going very slowly...
searching high and low.
Little Badger saw the moonlight glow.

"Hurrah!" he cried. "It's Sister Belle!"

"Oh, *there* you are, Little Badger,"
cried Sister Belle. "Where have
you been?"

"I couldn't find you, Sister Belle.
Then I got frightened and Dark was
coming," whispered Little Badger.

"You had no need to be afraid," smiled Sister Belle. "A badger learns to like the dark."

"Yes," said Little Badger. "I like it now. I'll never be afraid again."

The moon came up behind the trees. The dark went out of the big wood.

Then Sister Belle said, "This way, Little Badger!"

And she took him home.

Picture Ladybird

Books for reading aloud with 2–6 year olds

The exciting *Picture Ladybird* series includes a wide range
of animal stories, funny rhymes, and real life adventures that are
perfect to read aloud and share at storytime or bedtime.

A whole library of beautiful books for you to collect

RHYMING STORIES

Easy to follow and great for joining in!

Jasper's Jungle Journey, Val Biro
Shoo Fly, Shoo! Brian Moses
Ten Tall Giraffes, Brian Moses
In Comes the Tide, Valerie King
Toot! Learns to Fly,
Geraldine Taylor & Jill Harker
Who Am I? Judith Nicholls
Fly Eagle, Fly! Jan Pollard

IMAGINATIVE TALES

Mysterious and magical, or just a little shivery

The Star that Fell, Karen Hayles
Wishing Moon, Lesley Harker
Don't Worry William, Christine Morton
This Way Little Badger, Phil McMylor
The Giant Walks, Judith Nicholls
Kelly and the Mermaid, Karen King

FUNNY STORIES

Make storytime good fun!

Benedict Goes to the Beach, Chris Demarest
Bella and Gertie, Geraldine Taylor
Edward Goes Exploring, David Pace
Telephone Ted, Joan Stimson
Top Shelf Ted, Joan Stimson
Helpful Henry, Shen Roddie
What's Wrong with Bertie? Tony Bradman
Bears Can't Fly, Val Biro
Finnigan's Flap, Joan Stimson

REAL LIFE ADVENTURE

Situations to explore and discover

Joe and the Farm Goose,
Geraldine Taylor & Jill Harker
Going to Playgroup,
Geraldine Taylor & Jill Harker
The Great Rabbit Race, Geraldine Taylor
Pushchair Polly, Tony Bradman

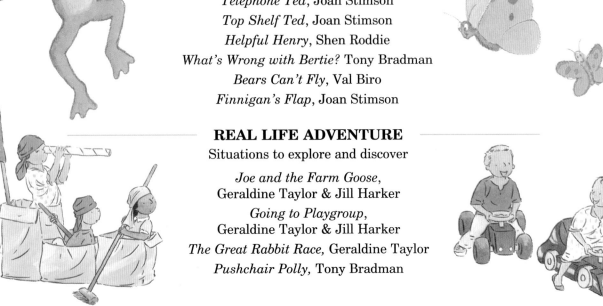